SUMMARY Of

Dr. Gundry's Diet Evolution:

Turn Off the Genes That Are Killing You and Your Waistline

By Steven R. Gundry

**Proudly Brought To You By
OneHour Reads**

Disclaimer

This book is a summary and meant to be a great companionship to the original book or to simply help you get the gist of the original book. If you're looking for the original book, kindly go to Amazon website, and search for the keyword Dr. Gundry's Diet Evolution: Turn Off the Genes That Are Killing You and Your Waistline.

Table of Contents

EXECUTIVE SUMMARY

In *Dr. Gundry's Diet Evolution*, Steven Gundry records his ground breaking discovery on how to lose weight, keep fit, and generally live a healthy life. His theory premises on the fact that our genes are responsible for the unhealthy eating habits that have brought about countless chronic diseases plaguing man today.

Our genes play a fundamental role in determining how we eat in the first place. Basically, they enforce on us a diet that ensures their own survival, while destroying our bodies. Gundry proposes a new way of restoring optimum health and total wellbeing: reprogramming our genes by eating right. He advocates the ideal diet as one reminiscent of what our earliest ancestors ate.

The book addresses distinct phases of his program: Doing away with the wrong foods; eating the right ones; and disabling what Gundry calls "Killer Genes"

His knowledge defies and transcends most of conventional understanding and may take some getting used to, but the author takes his time to trace the scientific foundations of his assertions, and share success stories of his diet program.

This is a good read if you've been trying, without success, to lose weight, maintain it and remain healthy.

CHAPTER 1: YOUR GENES ARE RUNNING THE SHOW

KEY TAKEAWAYS:

- *Your genes control you;*
- *Conventional food is bad for us and good for our genes;*
- *Killer genes are triggered by specific behaviors and they initiate disease and death*

It's often said: "Back to Basics", and in this case, genes are the basics. Before interrogating your diet, you need to have the right knowledge about your genes and the role they play in your diet, health, and overall wellbeing. Many of us know that the genes we get from our parents are responsible for how we look, how we talk, specific attitudes, etc. but we remain ignorant concerning the roles they play in so many other areas of our lives. As absurd or unbelievable as it may sound, our genes deceive us into eating the wrong things and damaging our health. It's good for them but bad for us. Weird, right?

The relationship between our genes and our bodies can be likened to how a computer operating system is basically the force behind that computer. Our genes- activated or deactivated by food substances- hold information that instructs each cell on what to do at every point in time. Our genes are housed inside our bodies, and without their direction, we do not function, much like the computer and its operating system. As our bodies evolve, so do our genes, as this is necessary for their survival, and that is really all what the genes look out for.

It might seem quite defeating but the truth is that, much of what we do, say think, feel, how we age, etc. are controlled by something fundamentally beyond our control. If you're in doubt, decide right now to hold your breath and see for how long that lasts. Eventually, you're *forced* to resume breathing. This is because you not breathing does no good for your genes, so they disapprove of your actions and do not *allow* it. Basically, our bodies are on auto-pilot, controlled by specific gene-carrying cells. When we do the expected things- like breathing- everything goes on smoothly. But when we veer off and decide not to breathe for instance, we can get hurt.

Your genes are concerned about preservation, for themselves. They could care less about you, really. So they point you in three major directions, which are ultimately aimed at reproduction. When you reproduce, they are transferred and preserved.

- They drive you to get as much energy- in form of calories- with as little exertion as possible. The implication of this is glaring: excess calories + minimal activity = too much weight or obesity. Interestingly, your genes shut down when they detect you're getting more than you should. That's why obesity kills.
- They drive us to stay away and run from pain

- They drive us to seek pleasure- mating rituals, sexual intimacy, and other pleasure-inducing substances like addictive drugs and the world's commonest vice today, Sugar.

So basically, they want you to reproduce and preserve copies of your own genes, and they also want you not to waste too much time hanging around; in their opinion, it's not ideal that you struggle for resources with younger ones. According to your genes, the more pleasurable (high-calorie) foods you eat, the higher your chances at surviving long enough to reproduce. And as you grow older, and your genes register this, your body will begin to deteriorate, telling you how you cannot continue to eat as much as the young ones.

Our genes are so intentional about their rules that whenever they detect threatening situations, they activate programmed responses to address the threats. You may not know, but there are more miscarriages of male unborn babies than female during food shortages. It's simple. Females are the ones designed to reproduce, so the more females, the more offspring, and continued preservation of genes. This is quite incredible, but this is how our genes work. Similarly, when you're the one threatening those rules, they take action, initiating what is called Killer Genes. They are so called because their job is to take out anyone they detect is competing unduly for scarce resources. They are a fundamental component in the human process of aging and death. So for instance, if you keep piling on the calories and are not keeping active enough, you become overweight, and the killer genes are alerted. Much the same way, when human activity decreases as a result of age advancement, the genes interpret it as you consuming useful resources when you can do little or nothing to contribute to the ecosystem. Over-stretching your body with rigorous exercise as well as smoking are also behaviors which trigger specific reactions and these reactions signal to your genes that you're not fit for existence. They- killer genes- inevitably swing into action.

Most of the foods we're in love with today, are instruments in the ultimate goals of our genes. They- our genes- want us to eat these foods so we can reproduce, after which they can do away with us, but this book provides the knowledge to outsmart them. The western world's diet is predominantly refined carbs, the reason for most of the peculiar diseases plaguing us- obesity, diabetes, heart-related diseases, and cancer. These foods hurt our bodies but our genes are happy with them. Why? They speed up our growth, make it possible to start childbearing at younger ages, and eventually, wipe us out to make room for the next generation. So, basically, birth rates increase, and so do early deaths, facilitated by a myriad of the aforementioned diseases.

Killer genes are responsible for triggering destructive changes in our body; changes that are meant to kill their target, or at least get them closer to death. For instance, eating too much of fats has often been pinned as the cause of heart attacks, but if there are arteries throughout or bodies, why is it only the heart's that is blocked? Simple.

Because our heart is very vital to the overall functioning of our bodies, and killer genes now just where to strike the heaviest blows.

Once killer genes are initiated by any of the identified behaviors, their sole aim is to destroy the human. Once the process is begun, a million and one disease could strike out their victim. They keep attacking, coming from different angles, weakening the body, until eventually the body gives up. That is why most obese folks also come with a whole bouquet of risks like diabetes, heart diseases, and cancer.

Usually, our bodies have ways of alerting us to the steady approach of killer genes, but the common response is wrong. We'd rather seek to address the symptoms than the root cause. And sadly, this does not solve the problem. You'll only end up taking a ton of medicine because the symptoms will be one too many; remember, the killer genes keep attacking.

The workings of killer genes help us to see how disease and death work. But it's not enough or right to run with the notion of genes as the ultimate bad guys. Yes, they are called killer genes, but really, they are only part of a programmed system that controls our body functioning. Most important to note is that you can get your genes to veer off the destructive path and place them firmly on the path to your health and general wellbeing.

CHAPTER 2: WE ARE WHAT WE EAT

KEY TAKEAWAYS:

- *Our ancestors ate food rich in nutrients and low in calories*
- *The volume of food we eat today is still largely the same as our ancestors ate*
- *The quality of food we eat today is greatly reduced*
- *The low-nutrient, high-calories diet popular today is responsible for rapid growth and reproduction- which our genes like- as well as rapid aging, diseases and death*
- *The ideal diet is one which is predominantly plant and supplemented by animal protein*

Why did our grandparents and great-grandparents not suffer from chronic diseases as much as we are doing today? How did we come from where they were with nutrition, to where we are now? These days, obesity has become a very common condition in our Western world, much more than in other parts of the world. Something has gone horribly wrong with our diets and general way of life, because for some reason, majority of our population seem to have initiated their killer genes. How did we get to this point?

Let's look at the chimps, gorillas, and apes. In the line of evolution, we're closest to them, so we share similarities in our diets. Plants- leaves and fruits- are a staple of their diet. For so long, we've all been told that calories mean nutrients. How erroneous! Calories do not indicate how nutritious a food is. The vitamins and minerals, and a bunch of other substances within the food make up its nutritional package. Apes have to consume a lot of leaves every day, unlike carnivorous animals, who do not eat as much because it's not as easy to chase down prey as it is to find plants and trees. In that sense, both the herbivorous and carnivorous animals spend little energy in getting their food, which is to the advantage of the genes.

Carnivorous animals sleep a lot because they ate more often, they would have to pay dearly for eating a lot of meat, which are very high in calories. The best source of calories is not animal protein, and at the end of the day, they feed on the herbivorous animals, which in turn feed on plants.

Our ancestors evolved to go beyond the Ape diet of leaves and fruit. They added meat, and from fossil evidence, that diet suited their bodies very well. The combination of meat and plants was so nutritious that humans evolved to stop producing essential nutrients like Vitamin C and B12. We were eating meat rich in Vitamin B12 and plants rich in Vitamin C, so our genetic combination created to manufacture those nutrients stopped functioning. Our ancestors passed those traits unto us; we cannot produce Vitamin C and B12. Sadly, our diet today is very different from what our Paleolithic ancestors fed on. We have made a sharp U-turn from their nutrient-rich, calories-meagre diet, and are now heavy consumers of refined grains and sugar (a lot!). Even the meat we consume are not the same they ate. Ours are commercially-raised on more grains and lack the rich nutrients contained in cows that fed on natural pasture. So yes, the quality of our contemporary diet is way lower than the diets enjoyed by our ancestors.

Interestingly- and quite unfortunately for us- the amount of food we eat today is not much different from that of the early mean and women. In other words, we're eating the same amount of food they ate, but not the same quality of food they ate. While our genes are enjoying it, this reality continues to spell doom for our bodies. Our genes are having a merry time with all the foods we're feeding them today, unlike with the early men and women who ate more of plants, supplemented by meat.

The downward spiral began about a thousand decades ago when it became apparent that we needed to cultivate food if we wanted to get enough for everybody. Man could no longer rely on wild hunting and gathering, hence, agriculture. It became possible to raise our own animals and plants. The discovery of grains was also very welcome. If man was happy, we had no idea how happier our genes were. Grains had a lot of nutrients but they had a lot of calories too. Agriculture, on the other hand, was soon deemed stressful, and wham! We introduced machines which helped us conserve our energy. So we were eating high-calorie foods and doing less work: perfect signal for killer genes.

The reality of inadequate resources is not lost on us, but somehow, our systems are tuned to keep seeking calories.

Our genes require micronutrients that are so scarce in contemporary diet, so they keep pushing us to eat until we find those nutrients. But we keep eating, and using less energy, thereby triggering killer genes.

We can learn a lot from wild animals. For one, you won't find any of them obese. They have a system that shuts down any feelings of hunger once they have enough stored in their bodies. They also eat foods rich in micronutrients so their genes are not compelled to seek out any more than necessary. Another factor that helps them stay satisfied is how long or how short their daytime is. Plus, specific cells produce hormones that order them to stop eating when they've had enough. It would interest you to know that you carry this ability too. It's no surprise that you don't know though. Today's giant food and pharmaceutical industry cannot benefit from you being informed.

In the old times, our ancestors went through gene modifications to help them survive in times of scarce resources needed for survival. In time, these modifications became regular, protecting their bodies from degenerating in dire times. Only then can we preserve our genes and transfer them to offspring.

Plants are another part of the big puzzle, and you'd be marvelled at the intricate design with which they ensure their protection and preservation. For one, they manufacture fruit that appeal to animals, who eat the fruits. But life resides in the seed, and that is needed for continued existence. So what do plants do? They concentrate a lot of poisonous substances in the seed, making it inedible for animals. They also concentrate these substances in their leaves, seeing that it provides the necessary energy for survival. You're probably wondering if these poisonous substances are present in the vegetables we eat. Yes. But because our ancestors have been eating plants since forever, our genes have evolved to develop a resistance to those substances. The liver plays a major role in this defence mechanism.

But there are plants with seeds that cannot be digested. They preserve by species by having you eat a lot of their indigestible seeds and excreting the same. In their new location, fortified by your body waste, they start life anew. They're quite smart and have a smart system to ensure that you eat a lot of their fruit. They simply secrete fructose, the sugar contained in fruit. This 'sugar', unlike glucose, prevents your brain from getting the message that you're filled up, so you don't feel full and you keep on eating. This fructose in your body system is responsible for producing cholesterol.

In the early days, this fructose strategy worked out well for both parties. It made sure animals ate a lot and had a full store of energy as fats when winter came and there was less food. This trait is what drives our genetic composition. We find sugary food and eat non-stop because our genes believe we need to stock up for the period of scarcity. But that is not what obtains in today's world. Yes, we have winter, but we still have food *in* winter. That's a problem, because we keep eating. We don't stop. And our genes approve because sugar-laden foods give the most calories with the very least effort.

But there are also plants without poisonous substances or fructose weapon. They protect and preserve their specie by producing substances that make it difficult to absorb nutrients. Bean seeds for example, release Phytates which perform such function. Before long, animals began to avoid it and similar seeds.

Fortunately, we have evolved over time to develop resistance to such defence strategies, even growing to benefit from them. Basically, plants, or vegetables, are good for us because they're not very good for our genes. They do not exactly aid the gene goals earlier listed.

Now, there's been a lot of argument over whether meats or vegetables are the real deal. Research shows that children who eat more vegetables don't grow or reproduce as rapidly as those who eat more meat. The former have also been found to live longer. But are vegetables really the winner in this war? And is this a case of winner takes all? Truth is, you should not have to choose between one and the other. Both are necessary for optimum growth and development. In the case of meat however, caution is advised, which means it is best to take it in small quantities. Why exactly is this? Meat requires a high rate of metabolism to be broken down into the form your body can use. This process speeds up aging, something those not-so-nice genes will be happy about.

No thanks to our fundamental programming, we find ourselves naturally craving sugary, salty, and fatty foods. On their own, there's nothing wrong with these, but when they become too much as a result of insatiable craving, trouble sets in. This trouble is what is manifested in so many chronic diseases affecting mankind today.

The word "Sugar" describes fragments of simple carbohydrate. They store energy, and when you have more than one of these fragments together, you get what is called a complex carbohydrate. So when you eat rice, which is carbohydrate, it eventually breaks down into sugars. Plants carry their largest deposits of sugar in the fruits and seeds. You already know why there's a lot of sugar in the fruit: to get you bingeing!

This suits animals just fine; after all, it's what the genes want. Even our tongues are designed to crave sugar. In the days of our ancestors, the most sugar was found in fruits, and that was natural. In the modern world however, there are a million and one sugary foods. In fact, we can say there is an entire sugar industry continuously rolling out sugary stuff that gladdens the genes and damages our bodies. To take charge of this dangerous trend, we will need to learn how to reprogram our systems. As uncomfortable as it might be, one of the most basic things you must accept in this journey is that once it's sweet, you need to exercise caution.

Our system is also programmed to crave fat, and although it is mostly seen as a bad thing, fats are actually very necessary in some ways. For one, many of the essential vitamins we get from food can only be absorbed in the presence of fat. Our ancestors got their fat from uninhibited animals; animals that ate grass and leaves. Unlike today's animals that are fed on grains, these ones provide us with omega-3 and omega-6 essential fats, which our bodies need but cannot produce.

Asides herbivores that feed on leaves and grass, algae-eating fish, like the wild salmon, are also rich in omega-3 fats. Omega-6 fats, on the other hand, can be found mostly in grains and seeds. Our bodies need both omega-3 and omega-6 but only in a balanced proportion. Omega-3 fatty acids however hold more benefit for our bodies; two omega-3 fats, DocosaHexanoic Acid (DHA) and EicosaPentaendic Acid (EPA) are very key in optimum mental health. More than that, omega-3 fatty acids produce anti-inflammatory hormones while omega-6 produces inflammatory hormones. That figures!

Our ancestors had it good because they ate the right kinds of food that gave them a balanced helping of both essential fats. Sadly, we are losing out on that. We are eating less plants (veggies) and meat fed on grass. We are eating meat fed with grain and oils made from grains. Omega-6 overload. It's no wonder there's been a rise in diseases like lupus, asthma, and a host of others.

Just as we are programmed to be on the lookout for sweet foods, so also our natural inclinations tend towards salt and salty foods. This condition is not completely out of place. It is only our body's answer to the necessity of salt for our survival. If our blood or cells did not get enough required salt, they would pack up. But the salt in today's diet does more than keep our bodies functioning. It kills our bodies. There's just too much salt in our foods today and our bodies were not made to handle that. If you're serious about this wellness journey, then exercise caution when you taste salt in your food.

Sugar, salt, and fat. We carry a natural inclination to these three things. It's no wonder that our contemporary society is so hooked on junk, which usually contains one or more of the three. Our genes are happy because our diets promote rapid reproduction- girls are maturing faster than ever before- while our bodies are rapidly deteriorating.

To a large extent, the discovery of grains triggered a downward trend. What's worse, flour was discovered as a refined product of grain, but that refining stripped flour of the fiber and oils present in grain. The result at the time was an astronomical increase in diseases. Why? Because refined grains turned out to be worse than chugging down heaps of table sugar. It released an unprecedented amount of sugar into blood streams, and it's still causing damage today.

CHAPTER 3: CHANGING THE MESSAGE

KEY TAKEAWAYS:

- *You can re-engineer your genes by sending them the right messages*
- *Diet evolution advocates not just weight loss but overall wellbeing*

So now we know that our default programming doesn't really advocate the best life for us. In our present reality, cravings for sugar, fat, and salt wreak more havoc than take a shot at preservation. We know that excess sugars are what is converted to fats by our bodies. We also know that we may have inherited the wrong set of genes from our ancestors, making our weight gain not entirely our fault. But here's the thing: we *CAN* make new guidelines for our genes. We are not helpless. It will take some work on our part, but we can rewrite the story.

So far, the diet and general lifestyle you've kept have been communicating specific messages to your genes. Those messages are responsible for how your gene reacts- to build you or tear you down. To make a U-turn, you won't need to get new genes. No, that's not how it works. You'll still have the same set of genes, but because you'll be eating the right foods (for you) and adopting the right lifestyle (again, for you), there will be a different set of messages being sent to your genes. These new messages will make it possible for you to lose weight and be healthy generally. You need to stop eating the foods your genes want you to eat.

Diet evolution is very much unlike most diet plans. Because it is built on the foundation of our evolutionary diet, it has nothing to do with strict measurements and complex classifications. Our ancestors did not know to eat fifty percent plants or forty percent fats. They just ate. Diet evolution helps you lose weight almost effortlessly. You only need to follow a few simple, easy-to-recollect rules, measuring tips, food lists, and a bathroom scale.

A lot of diet routines have good intentions. The problem is that they often require people to adopt strange eating habits, marking a brisk departure from what one has been used to for so long. Nothing- absolutely nothing- can be successfully learned that way. The key is to take it one step at a time, easing in new habits and edging out old, unhealthy ones. This is the approach taken by Diet Evolution. Eventually, you'll find it seamless to become an expert at handling your genes the right way to give you optimum health.

Your first step will be to put a stop to all the wrong messages you've been sending your killer genes, and in effect, turning them off. That will help you lose weight, but that will not help you sustain the weight loss and an overall healthy lifestyle. A next step will be embarked upon to undo all the havoc that killer genes have wreaked on your system, while also working towards overall health renewal.

The program will also take you through the process of unlearning many of the untruths you've been fed. So, get ready to be shocked, for your own good. Some of those myths include:

- Fable: Oatmeal is good for the heart
  Truth: Eating refined grains is worse than eating sugar
- Fable: Banana's potassium makes it a health food
  Truth: Ripe bananas highly increase your blood sugar
- Fable: orange juice contains a lot of vitamins
  Truth: Orange juice is just a ton of sugars
- Fable: Low-calorie and Zero-calorie sweeteners are good for weight loss
  Truth: Any type of sweetener is worse than sugars.

Also, there are a few things you need to keep in mind as you take this bold step. They will help keep you grounded on your journey:

- The phytochemicals manufactured by plants exist to protect them from predators and destruction; for preservation.
- Evolution of animal genes occurred in interaction with plant phytochemicals.
- You NEED these phytochemicals for proper functioning of your cells.
- The agenda of your genes are not supported by plant leaves and seeds, so yes, they're good for you.
- Conventional food advance the goals of your genes so they're bad for your health.

- Refined grain products fill your blood with sugar, which is converted to excess fats, and bad for your health.
- Conventional foods are highly concentrated with omega-6 fats, which produce inflammatory hormones.

CHAPTER 4: THE DIET AT A GLANCE

KEY TAKEAWAYS:

- *The three phases of diet evolution will require you sending the right messages to your genes*
- *Each phases of the program runs seamlessly into the next*
- *Exercise and supplements are a fundamental part of the program*

Before commencing Diet evolution, it is advisable to run some tests and speak to your physician. This will help you tailor the program to your specific medical status, and ensure that you achieve maximum results. You should consider taking the following tests:

- Fasting glucose level
- Hemoglobin A1C
- Fasting insulin level
- Fasting lipid panel
- Homocysteine
- Fibrinogen
- C-reactive protein (CRP)

The program consists of three distinct phases, all with markedly different eating patterns and exercise regimen. In those three phases, you will be changing the narrative you have sold your genes for so long, which have turned them against you.

Phase 1:

You will convince your genes that there's no need to store up fats. During this phase, you're aiming to lose some weight, so you'll completely avoid refined grains, sugar, and processed foods. Your main diet will consist of lots and lots of vegetables and proteins like meat and poultry. If you're craving snacks, eat nuts and seeds. You can run this phase for about six weeks, that is, if you don't have any chronic weight problems.

Phase 2:

Your message to your genes here should be that you're not useless, so that they do not initiate the process of finishing you off. Increase the veggies and decrease the meat. Eat only certain fruits. Continue snacking on nuts and seeds. You can explore with some whole grain and beans too, but only in the littlest sizes. You can stay in this phase for about six weeks as well.

Phase 3:

Finally, you'll want to tell your genes that you're better off alive for their sakes. This is the time to take only minimal portions of animal protein and eat as many low-calories raw veggies as you can. Stay away from legumes and whole grains. The more plant nutrients you consume, the more you'll resemble your ancestors who lived long, healthy lives. This process turns on the genes that protect and preserve you. Now you're on your way to total health and wellbeing.

These phases will give you a seamless transition that will make it less difficult to change your old habits and adopt new ones.

Another major part of the program is exercise, and for so long, we have been hyping the wrong thing. This program will provide just the ones to pass across the right messages to our genes. You must be ready to take the right supplements as well. They will augment your efforts in the other components. You need supplements not just because you cannot access all the plant foods our ancestors ate, but also because the vegetables we eat today are not the ones they ate. Most of our vegetables are mass-produced plants steeped in pesticides, chemical fertilizers, and other chemical substances.

The following are some of the foods you can eat:

- PROTEINS
  - Pasture-fed meat
  - Free-range poultry
  - Wild fish
- DAIRY
  - Fresh cheese
  - Aged cheese
  - Eggs
  - Kefir
- SOY AND OTHER PROTEINS
  - Tofu
  - Edamame
  - Tempeh

- VEGGIES
  - Leafy greens
  - Zucchini
  - Carrots
  - Water chestnuts
  - Onions
  - Artichokes
  - Olives
  - Cauliflower
  - Brussels sprouts
  - Peppers
- OILS
  - Extra-virgin olive oil
  - Flaxseed oil
  - Macadamia nut oil
  - Walnut oil
- SEASONING
  - Salt and pepper
  - Tomato sauce or paste
  - Spices and herbs
  - Soy sauce
  - Lemon and lime juice
- SEEDS AND NUTS
  - Macadamia nuts
  - Almonds
  - Pistachios
  - Hemp seeds
  - Sesame seeds
- FOOD SUBSTITUTES

- Rice protein powder
- Low-carb protein bars and shakes
- BEVERAGES
  - Green tea
  - Red wine
  - Black tea

Some of the foods you should stay away from are:

- Veggies
  Sweet potatoes, cooked corn, yams
- White foods
  Mayonnaise, white bread, frozen yoghurt, sugar
- Beige foods
  Cookies, cereals, French fries
- Dangerous fruits
  Pineapple, banana, grapes, dates, dried fruit
- Soda, fruit juices, and vegetable juices
- All kinds of sweeteners

At the onset of your program, you need to do away completely with foods such as Barley, Millet, Rye, Legumes, etc. They make weight loss pretty difficult so they're not the foods you want to be eating. As you progress into the second phase, you'll be able to reincorporate them into your diet. They're also not the best for weight loss, which is why they're prohibited from Phase 1, but even in Phase 2, they should only be eaten minimally. Such fruits include:

- Blackberries
- Strawberries

- Avocado
- Apple
- Grapefruit
- Cherries, etc.

If you have cause to eat out while on your program, do not slip into your old ways. Self-enforce rules such as nibbling on salads instead of an entrée and eating berries for dessert.

Phase 1: THE TEARDOWN
Chapter 5: THE FIRST TWO WEEKS

KEY TAKEAWAYS:

- *This stage is very pivotal to the success of your entire program*
- *A high-protein, high-vegetable diet is used to transmit new messages to your genes and induce weight loss*
- *Protein provides the calories while vegetables provide the micronutrients*
- *Sugar in all forms is the enemy*
- *Avoid processed foods*
- *Bacteria are an essential part of this stage*

This first stage is much like peeling old paint off a house before applying a new coat. You'll eat a lot of vegetables and get your calories from approved protein. Avoid deep-frying or cooking your foods too much, and if you're going to use some oil on your veggies, use olive or canola. The problem with most diets is that they skip this foundational stage. This is the stage at which you turn around the messages you've been feeding your genes, letting them know there's no need to store fat. Bottom line is, if you ignore this phase, you'll find it difficult to sustain any diet changes you make later on. It's like you getting the soil ready for planting. You get to do it only for some time, before work starts.

The vegetables and proteins you'll eat in these two weeks will be in proportion of More to Less, meaning you'll eat more of vegetables and very little protein, preferably not more than the size of your palm. Remember that the best vegetables are the leafy, green ones. You also get to snack minimally on nuts and seeds. If you're not cool with the animal protein, you could substitute with any of the following:

- Cottage cheese
- Swiss cheese
- Almond milk (plain)
- Yoghurt (plain and unsweetened)
- Free-range eggs
- Tofu

Eating animal protein at this stage is reminiscent of your ancestors who ate a lot of animal protein during winter, when there were no plants and they had to survive. In other words, you're tricking your genes into believing it is dry season and you need to burn fat, not store it. Another upside to the protein inclusion at this stage is that proteins require a lot of energy to be digested by your body.

In other words, you lose a lot of calories producing heat when your body tries to absorb protein. Lost calories equals weight loss, so, there you have it! But that's not all, the heat production itself stimulates a feeling of fullness, ultimately helping you to eat less and not aggravate your genes.

Remember we started this phase with a Vegetable-Protein combination. You know now what the protein helps you with. Vegetables, on the other hand, provide you with much needed nutrients, the kinds your ancestors fed on so long ago. Because vegetables are such a darling, you can eat as much as you want; you don't have to stop till you're full. Just make sure you're eating the right ones. The leafier they are, the better. The greener they are, the better. Eat a lot as raw salads and resist the urge to cook, except if absolutely necessary. Best part, you can eat it anytime- breakfast, lunch, or dinner, or even every time. And if that is not so good news for you, no biggie. Just take your time and gradually increase your intake portions. You really need the veggies, a variety of them. There are more than one leafy greens you can find, and even some that are not so leafy but do your body good all the same.

Eating your vegetables will work maximally if you also include snacks of seeds and nuts, or both. Drinking 8-10 glasses of water also helps. You may even spice things up with some red wine or pure spirits.

Another thing to note during this stage is that eating foods- animal or plant- high in protein is not the same as eating food high in fats. Protein helps you shed calories while fat has not been proven beneficial.

So far, you have read that you can snack on seeds and nuts, but what exactly do they do for you? First off, the human brain will always seek glucose because that is its preferred source of energy, but because this stage allows zero carbs and sugar, that glucose is not readily available. But the brain is relentless. It goes raiding throughout your body for the glucose, and this raid could get it to strip other body parts of their nutrients. One of those parts is your muscle. Draining glucose from your muscle is one of the mechanisms through which a zero-sugar diet causes you to quickly lose weight, but it can also be harmful for your body, because you don't need our muscle collapsing. Nuts and seeds release protein and glucose in small quantities. That glucose satisfies your brain to an extent and keeps it from looking in and stripping the wrong places of useful nutrients.

Nuts and seeds also reduce hunger pangs, ultimately helping you to eat less. Just do well to stay away from salted nuts and seeds, or any processed stuff generally. It sort of defeats the entire process, doesn't it?

One of the pillars of this phase is a complete ban on sugar, but this is also maybe one of the most difficult things to achieve. You already know how our brains are wired to seek out sugar, salt, and fat. Since you know the enemy and the power it wields, and how your body is also a traitor in the mix, you should know how much work you have cut out for you. Fortunately, you can augment your efforts by taking supplements that have been proven to reduce sugar cravings. Selenium, Chromium, and Cinnamon spice are three of such effective supplements.

Another necessary component of this stage is the replenishing of bacteria in your body. Don't get scared. It's the right kind of bacteria, such as L. rhamnosus and Bifidobacterium bifidum that you need. You need the benefits derived from these bacteria, especially if you've been taking antibiotics and eating the wrong kinds of food. You can find supplements containing these helpful bacteria and use them.

But they need to be used alongside what is called prebiotics. The best form of prebiotics are Fructo-OligoSaacharides, but you can just call them FOS. They help you perform three functions:

- Reducing your cholesterol level
- Taking in more calcium and magnesium
- Boosting your immune system

You'll find FOS in onions, yacon, artichokes, garlic, etc.

CHAPTER 6: WHAT'S OFF THE MENU?

KEY TAKEAWAYS:

- *The reason you're avoiding certain foods is because they activate killer-genes*
- *Fruits and milk are not always healthy for you*
- *Fruit and vegetable juices are purely sugar and have no nutritional value*
- *Take your progress with the phase slow and steady*
- *Give your body time to adjust to your new eating routine*
- *The ultimate goal is to eat as our ancestors did*

You've seen the foods you should eat and why, but you also need to know why you shouldn't eat the foods you're advised to avoid. Of course, it's no easy task saying goodbye to these foods. For one, your brains are wired to want them. Two, they are the easiest and cheapest food items to get in today's world- soda, Ice-cream, fruit juice, candy, pasta, you name it. But if you're on this program, then your ultimate goal is to move successfully through the phases until you're at a place where your diet is similar to what your ancestors ate way before agriculture and commercial production of food.

The first stage is very essential, which is why you'll be cutting off a lot, including

- Fruits
- Cooked carrots and the like
- Legumes- lentils, beans, and what not

Foods categorized as White and Beige are the enemy because they tell your genes to store fat. Eating carbs and sugar informs your genes that you're in the season of plenty; that you have an abundance of sugar-laden fruits at your disposal, and that you need to store up fat for winter/dry season. And if there's anything that must be achieved in this phase, it is the reworking of your messages to your genes.

You need to avoid sugar to lead them into believing it is wintertime, and that they need to burn fat. At this stage, you'll do well to avoid everything that contains carbs and sugars of any kind. Don't bother buying organic bread or pasta either. They still send the same signals to your genes; the signals that cause your genes to turn against you.

High-carb and sugary foods are usually easier to explain away, but what you might frown at is the instruction to avoid fruit. Yes, fruit! You've been told all your life that it's good to eat fruits, but the truth is that they still send the wrong signals to your genes. They send exactly the same message as sugars and starches. In these first two weeks, avoid all kinds of fruits. You can reincorporate them into your diet after this first phase.

Fruit and vegetable juices are worse, and should be avoided altogether. You don't want to continue putting this in your body system at all. Why? After all, they are from fruit, right? Wrong? These juices are best described as sugar in a bottle. Yes, they come packed with more sugars, most of which are not natural.

In this large umbrella of sugar, artificial sweeteners also reside. As such, you should do all you can to avoid them as well.

Another food which may not sound reasonable to avoid, is milk. For so long, we have been bombarded with messages about how fabulous milk is, but it would surprise you to know that our bodies are not built to absorb milk past infancy. Majority of humans are lactose-intolerant, and the few who are not are as a result of mutation. Naturally, adults shouldn't be drinking milk. It's more dangerous because milk contains a hormone called IGF, which stimulates non-stop growth of cells, a major precursor of cancer.

IGF interacts with your liver as insulin, increasing your blood sugar and informing your genes to store fat. If you're such a milk fan and you're thinking of drinking skimmed milk instead, you're only opting for a deadlier option, because skimmed milk contains more sugar and does more damage. Cheese, on the other hand, does not contain IGF, so you can get your protein from there without fear.

The standard duration for this first phase is two weeks, but that is not cast in stone. Because we do not all have the same medical conditions, and we may not be able to stick to the rules of the phase to the same extent, some may have to spend longer in this phase than others. That's fine. Besides, it's best to take things at a steady pace. After the rapid weight loss that usually attends the first phase it is not advisable to continue losing weight at such a tempo. That kind of weight loss is usually difficult to maintain, so it's no surprise that you see someone lose a lot of weight at once, only to gain it all back soon enough.

Your genes revolt after you've kept a low-calorie, low-carb streak for a while, and if there's no easing into the rebuilding phase, the hunger pangs they- your genes- stimulate will get you eating up all the pounds you've already lost. Worse still, losing a lot of weight too quickly triggers the release of poisonous substances in our bodies.

Bottom-line, don't beat yourself up over weight loss. Remember, weight loss is only one component of the Diet Evolution; it is not the entire thing. Besides, it's okay to go at your own pace.

Taking a variety of supplements including Magnesium, Vitamin E, and Folic Acid also help you on your journey. Another thing that will make this journey less gruelling is tolerating your own weaknesses. Most times, it's not easy switching from your preferred eating habits to these new ones, so who says you can't let yourself off the hook once in a while? For instance, if you're not really feeling the sugar-off, you can use a pinch of artificial sweetener in your beverages, or eat chocolate with over seventy percent concentration of cocoa.

After the two weeks originally earmarked for this phase, you might want to decide if you should move on or still stay on a little more. People do not lose weight the same way, and if you're not satisfied with your results, consider your:

- Individual weight situation
- Medical conditions such as diabetes

If you're ready to move on to the next stage, then there's some respite as your approved foods are less rigid.

CHAPTER 7: THE TEARDOWN CONTINUES

KEY TAKEAWAYS:

- *You can eat lentils and whole grains, but only minimally*
- *Berries, citrus, apples are some of the fruits you can eat at this stage*
- *Avoid completely, all kinds of dried fruit*
- *Gradually reduce your protein*
- *You actually need some kinds of fats*
- *Grain-based fats are unhealthy*
- *Natural foods are a good source of essential omega-3 fatty acids*

After the first two weeks of reprograming your genes and sending them the right message, you're probably already seeing results; losing weight and feeling better. With your next step, not only will you be making a few changes to your diet here and there, you will also be telling your genes- by the foods you eat- that their survival is tied to your continued existence. This will initiate a rebuilding process and get your genes to work for your wellbeing.

You can now introduce fruits, but only certain types. Cherries, berries, plums, and grapes are some of these fruits. Not only do they enhance long life, they also contain special antioxidants that boost brain functioning. Oranges, grapefruits, and apples also fall in this category. Just make sure not to overdo them and do not eat dried fruit. They are not the same.

The 'Brown' foods can also be introduced at this stage. Lentils, beans, and whole grains can be cooked and enjoyed, but only minimally (ideally, a half-cup serving). If you're very particular about weight loss however, your best bet is to stay away from them.

You should also reduce your protein intake in proportion to your vegetables. Eat more of vegetables and very little of protein. By this, you're toning down on calories and stocking up on micronutrients so richly found in vegetables.

When it comes to weight loss and optimum health, Glycemic Index and Glycemic Load are not as consequential as we've been made to believe. We certainly do not need to get paranoid over them as many diet fads claim. Fruits, brown, white, and beige foods are the main culprits to look out for in failure to lose weight or reduce cholesterol.

The fact that we have good and bad cholesterol- HDL and LDL- is common knowledge, but you probably are not aware that even those two categories carry sub-categories. For instance, only one of the five types of HDL actually purifies your arteries. Contrary to popular opinion that places all the blame at the feet of your genes, research has shown that the sugar and starches you consume are responsible for how high or low your cholesterol levels are, and the ratio of good to bad ones that you carry.

One particular type of cholesterol you do not want is lipoprotein (a), otherwise known as Lp (a). Basically, it increases the risk of premature coronary artery disease and is as deadly as can be. Research has shown however, that

Diet Evolution, combined with two specific supplements is able to overpower the Lp (a)- producing gene. This is not before you find out if you carry the gene though, so get tested.

It is a known fact that your triglyceride levels shoot up as you increase intake of brown, beige, and white foods, as well as fruits like ripe bananas and mangoes. Increased triglyceride means increased LDL cholesterol and weight gain. Yes, it's possible to eat high-calorie foods without gaining weight, but not at this level. The best you can do is stay away.

You've read about how grains revolutionized human diet when they were discovered. They were nothing short of a miracle at the time, but nowadays, they have turned the enemy and are pumping our blood full of sugar. A very good example is oats. Contrary to what the American Heart Association (AHA) and advert messages have told you, oats are nothing more than sugar foods. The only oats that are healthy are the ones that were eaten by generations way before ours. They were called steel oats and are nothing like the processed ones we eat today. Same goes for corn and legumes, so even if you want to eat them, make sure they are in very little portions.

Fats and oils can be introduced at this stage, but the trick is to use the healthy ones; the ones that will not send the wrong messages to your genes. Once upon a time, fat was the enemy, but now we know that we need some fats, such as omega-3 fatty acids. These fats are naturally found in small fish like sardines, and big fish like swordfish.

Basically, it is found in fish that feed on sea plants- like algae. It is also found in fish that feed on the plant-eating small fish. That is the natural order. Unfortunately, most of the fish that get to us today did not feed on the right things. Other sources of this essential fat include:

- Olive oil (extra-virgin)
- Hemp seeds
- Walnut
- Avocado

Unlike these sources, oils gotten from grains- soybean, corn, etc. - are mainly concentrated with omega-6 fats. Although your body needs both fats, it needs them in balanced quantities because while omega-3 fats reduce inflammation, omega-6 fats increase it. Unfortunately, the bulk of our foods today are grain-based. Yes, the readily-available meat, fish, and poultry are those raised commercially and fed with grains. That is why you need to be intentional about eating vegetables and the right kinds of oil. Besides, if you're going to eat protein, make sure your fish is wild, your poultry (including eggs) free-range, and your meat pasture-fed. Another advantage of omega-3 fats, which is very key to your Diet Evolution objectives, is that it puts a leash on your sugar cravings.

As usual, there is also the role of supplements. The following are only some of the supplements that can be incorporated in this stage of your journey:

- Mushroom extracts
- Cranberry extract
- Pycnogenols
- Magnesium, which helps manage hypertension
- Olive leaf extract
- Fish oil supplements
- Hempseed oil
- Flaxseed oil

Try not to forget these three things:

- Your ancestors did not eat grain-based oils. It didn't even exist during their time!
- Avoid modified foods. The more modified, the unhealthier
- The longer a food's shelf-life, the shorter it makes your life span

CHAPTER 8: SETTLING IN

KEY TAKEAWAYS:

- *Breaks are good for you*
- *Hunger pangs and cravings increase during these breaks*
- *Sleeping more helps you lose more weight*
- *Consult the dirty dozen for list of foods to avoid*
- *Moderate exercise is healthy*
- *Go at your own pace*

Before you run along with the euphoria of your weight loss and overall good feeling, you need to be aware of the fact that a time will come when these results will drastically reduce, or in some cases, stop altogether. It's easy to run with the assumption that, just like every other diet, this one has also failed you, but that is not the case. On the contrary, it is actually working! Your genes are responding to the new signals you've been sending them. So why the recess, you ask?

Simple. You have reached a saturation point of sorts. You need to take a break from the weight loss momentum so far if you care about sustainable results. It's like what is known in Yoga as "settling in". If you were to continue on that momentum, your genes would probably revolt with hunger pangs and cravings that will get you right back to where you started, or even worse.

There's no need to despair at this recess stage. All you need do is stay faithful to your new diet- more vegetables, less protein, nuts and seeds snacks, etc. in fact, one of the benefits of getting to this stage is that it can help you sustain the habits that have initiated weight loss. It's a step further towards stabilizing your weight.

In Yoga, you get to push the limits on poses you can achieve. When you hit a snag and your muscles do not seem to be cooperating anymore, masters often advise that you stay at the farthest point you can reach and just settle in, ignoring your uncooperative muscles and just breathing. Soon enough, your muscles eventually bend to your quiet will. That is how it is with Diet Evolution. When you reach that point where it seems you're not losing weight anymore and nothing is happening, just take your time to settle in. Get more familiar with your new diet that has brought you so far, and maintain it.

It is also likely that during this period, ghrelin, the hormone which stimulates hunger, is produced in larger quantities. This is especially more pronounced in summer, and it's a very natural reaction. To manage this, you can practice your settling in to keep yourself from yielding. Reducing the number of fruits you eat, exercising more, and sleeping more also help.

If you're wondering how more sleep helps, you're not alone. May people do not know that ghrelin, the hunger hormone is sensitive to light and how much sleep you get. When you sleep less, your genes assume you're in summer and proceed to store fat by increasing ghrelin levels. On the other hand, when you sleep more, your genes take it that you're in winter and proceed to burn fat instead. Besides, the more you sleep, the less you'll be eating.

If you're putting on more weight, chances are that you've relaxed and are now eating or sugary foods generally. Sometimes, it's not intentional. Misleading food labels can put you in a rut and get you eating the wrong things. A list called the dirty dozen identifies the pitfalls you should look out for. A few of those include:

- Sports bars, diet bars, or energy bars
- Sports drinks or vitamin waters
- Diet soda
- Sugar of any kind- natural sugar, organic sugar, syrups, etc.
- Fruit juice and canned vegetable

In addition to eating foods rich in omega-3 fatty acids to suppress hunger and unhealthy cravings, you can also use tested and trusted supplements like Citromax and St. John's Wort.

Exercise can be a great supplement too. Contrary to what many people think, it may not help you lose weight fast, but it offers a myriad of psychological benefits that can help you with settling in. Endorphins are secreted when you exercise and they serve to calm you. Exercise is good, as long as it does not require you exerting maximum strength. You don't want to tell your genes you're finding it difficult to survive. Tai chi and Yoga are good examples of helpful exercise.

Remember that, depending on your specific medical condition or just personal preference, you can choose to stay in a phase for as long as you want.

Phase 2: THE RESTORATION
CHAPTER 9: BEGIN THE RESTORATION

KEY TAKEAWAYS:

- *Your ideal diet should contain the least animal protein*
- *Green, leafy vegetables are the best*
- *Vegetables do contain protein and are packed with nutrients that animal protein lack*
- *Think "Main dish- vegetables; Side dish- animal protein"*

The goal in this stage is to get you eating like our long-time ancestors, the ones who lived before the discovery and practice of agriculture. So far, the diet in the first stage got you eating foods similar to how our more recent descendants did. In their case, they lived relatively better lives than us, but it was nothing compared to the lives of our early ancestors, who ate predominantly plants. They enjoyed a calorie sparse diet and that is what you should aim at if you want sustained weight control and overall wellbeing.

Don't be deceived by the tag "low-calorie" which is basically the coinage of manufacturers to deceive buyers. It does not mean the same thing a "calorie-sparse". As a matter of fact, low-calorie refined grains usually contain an insane amount of sugar. Basically, foods that are considered calorie-dense are those with large amounts of calories in their small quantity. This is where leaves prove without any doubt to be the healthiest choice. For instance, the calories present in about eight bags of romaine can be found easily in one tiny cube of cheese!

Going the raw and green route will see you eating mostly raw, green, leafy vegetables and you'll be the better for it. One of the functions of the micronutrients you get from vegetables is that they curb hunger; you feel full faster and eat less. The more leafy greens you eat, the less calories and more micronutrients your feed your genes. Even with your meat, poultry, or fish, notice how the healthy ones are those that fed on greens?

Not only do greens deliver the least calories, they also satisfy your genes in a very important way. Your genes require so many of the plant phytochemicals to perform specific important functions. For instance, Vitamin C is needed by your genes to prevent and repair wrinkles. What this means is that your genes will always need these nutrients. The more you eat them, the more satisfied your genes are. If you refuse to eat them however, your genes will continue to seek them, meaning you'll continue to bite from food to food until you find them. Bottom-line, you'll be eating more.

It would interest you to know that the fiber found in leafy greens is what speeds up the rate at which food travels through your lower bowel, triggering the release of anti-hunger hormones that tell you to stop eating. Research has shown that if you can eat one bag of dark leafy greens every day, not only will you be taking in less calories, you will also be making it clear to your genes that you are not a threat to the future generations.

At this stage, you should also phase out all the existing sources of calories in your diet- cheese, meat, and legumes. They served their purpose well enough in the first phase, but at this stage, the lesser you eat of them, the healthier for you. In the first phase, animal protein was a must-have, because you needed the high rate of metabolism and heat production it triggers to lose weight rapidly. But that was then, and unless you want your genes to pick up the signal that you're struggling, that metabolism rate is not one you want to keep up.

As you might have figured out already, this phase is about you evolving your diet- eating more calorie-sparse foods, greener, leafy vegetables; reducing animal protein, legumes, and grains. You should stay in this phase for at least six weeks. Your protein will begin to come mostly from vegetables, eggs and nuts. Plus, there are innumerable nutrients and phytochemicals from which you can benefit when you eat vegetables. Continue to avoid the foods classified as white or beige, and if you must legumes or whole grains, reduce it to the barest minimum. You can continue snacking on nuts and seeds in this stage.

Finally, reorient yourself to think of animal protein as side dish, lesser in size to your main dish, which should be a bouquet of green leaves.

CHAPTER 10: PICKING UP THE PACE

KEY TAKEAWAYS:

- *Exercise is a good way to maintain lost weight*
- *If you want to eat more calories, work for it!*
- *Strenuous exercise activate killer genes*
- *Moderate exercise that mimics the activities of our ancestors is considered ideal*
- *The right exercises help to reduce insulin*
- *Supplements play a part too*

In the overall scheme of things, exercise does not initiate weight loss, but it is useful in maintaining weight loss. Having gotten to this point, you must have lost some weight and come to a place where you can only consume considerably lesser calories. So what do you do if you want more? This is where exercise comes in.

If you want to eat more calories without putting your weight at risk, you'll have to work for it. Yes, work, similar to what your ancestors did to find and eat food in their days. But of course you know that the work (exercise) must not be too strenuous, else your genes interpret them as you struggling and not fit to exist anymore. It helps to pick exercise that can easily be metamorphose into habit.

Walking is one of those activities our early forebears did a lot of. This contrasts the erroneous belief that running is a heart-friendly exercise. Far from it! Running vigorously for long periods- either on a treadmill or on the tracks- expends too much energy and sends a dangerous signal to your genes, triggering killer genes.

Your ancestors also lifted heavy things, so lifting weights and doing chores that involve lifting will do you good.

Doing these things communicate to your genes that you're thriving and not threatening the future generation. You don't have to start big. You can work with your strength, do what you can handle for now, and watch your abilities increase.

Exercising the right way restores your muscle mass, which in turn reduces your insulin level, making it impossible for your genes to get the "store fat" signal, and also reduces the risk of cancer. Yes, you win!

Supplements are also a good way of complementing your exercise efforts towards rebuilding and sustaining muscle strength.

Phase 3: LONGEVITY
CHAPTER 11: THRIVING FOR A GOOD, LONG TIME

KEY TAKEAWAYS:

- *Raw, leafy vegetables are best*
- *Toxins in raw plants induce hormesis, a reaction that promotes longevity of life*
- *Ease gradually into the raw vegetables diet to avoid side effects*
- *With your vegetables, bitter is better*
- *Eat the 'strange' vegetables- like algae*

This final phase concentrates on getting you beyond the "weight loss" thinking to the "thriving life" mentality. As such, you will need to go back even farther in time, when your earliest ancestors did not know about cooking and ate their vegetables raw. As unpalatable as that may sound to you, it is an established fact that raw plants contain the highest concentration of nutrients and phytochemicals. They also help you consume lesser calories because they're bulkier. The amount of nuts and seeds snacks you eat must also be halved at this stage.

When our human body systems come in contact with low levels of poisonous and unfavourable substances not enough to harm us, we produce a response known as Hormesis. Interestingly, Hormesis makes a person more resistant to survival threats. When the unfavourable condition is aggravated though, killer genes are activated.

Eating lesser calories produces another instance of hormesis, and has been repeatedly proven by research to elongate life span. This is why mainly vegetables tend to be shorter but live longer. To deal with plant toxins, their genes initiate a process that inhibits them from growing and reproducing rapidly, thus living longer. Vegetables with a bitter taste are the ones that trigger this process the best. So, when choosing your vegetables, although you may not jump at it, remember bitter is better.

This new diet of yours will be enhanced by a couple of practices you should embrace. They'll also help you initiate hormesis, and ultimately, a longer, thriving life.

Cook less and less of your vegetables. Hormesis is induced by plant toxins, and you'll lose most of that with cooking. Like most new stuff, it will likely be challenging trying to switch to raw vegetables, so take your time to ease into it. You can even start by cooking your vegetables halfway to gradually get your taste buds used to raw veggies. You might also experience side effects from eating raw veggies, so you don't want to overdo it the first time. As you read earlier, slow and steady is the best.

Explore bitter vegetables if you want to unlock your longevity genes. Kale, collards, red and green cabbages, are some of the less popular vegetables. Sad, because they pack the most nutritional value. Try them. And you don't even have to eat them alone. You can spice things up with some lemon juice and olive oil. Yum!

Eat the 'weird' vegetables. Algae, Nori, and Seaweed are but a few of these uncommon but highly nutritious plants.

Eating only raw foods works wonders for your body, but not everyone can do it. Do not beat yourself if you find it hard to give 100% compliance. Do what you can at the moment, and continue to push your boundaries- at your own pace- to see just how farther you can go.

CHAPTER 12: TRICKING YOUR GENES: BEYOND DIET

KEY TAKEAWAYS:

- *Fasting induces hormesis*
- *So do coffee, tea, dark chocolate, red wine, exercise, and extreme temperatures*
- *After activating your longevity genes, you can cheat and still get away with it*
- *Freedom to cheat must be handled with responsibility*

You know by now that Hormesis is beneficial and can be induced when you get lesser amounts of calories. Basically, this means you can explore other ways of inducing hormesis, asides eating raw vegetables. One of such means is going without food for some period of time, or better still, fasting. How you do it is up to you. You may decide to go without food, eat unusually light, or skip one or two meals. But like everything else, do not overdo it.

Okay, so this may not be something you'll commit to with a smile on your face, but consider this. Your earliest ancestors had to walk miles to find food, and sometimes they didn't find food early enough. They would have had to skip breakfast on some days, or their hunting could have been unsuccessful on other days, making fasting necessary. Believe it or not, your genes are familiar with that.

So much talk about plant toxins inducing hormesis, but taking moderate doses of alcohol- specifically spirits and red wine- produces similar results. Not more than two daily servings for women and not more than three for men, is ideal. Because alcohol can be highly addictive, there is need to exercise caution with this. If you don't drink before now, don't pick up the habit for the sake of weight loss. It doesn't work that way.

Coffee and Tea (Black and Green) also induce hormesis, but they should be taken without milk. Dark chocolate too, as long as it contains at least 70% cocoa.

Exposure to extreme temperatures also produce stress, initiating hormesis and your longevity genes. So don't be too mad at the hot weather or the chilling colds. Apparently, they do you some good.

Exercising- not strenuously- is another activity that can activate your longevity genes.

Inducing hormesis and activating your longevity gene gives you freedom. Yes, by this phase, you have successfully gotten your genes to agree that you're valuable and should be preserved, so you can get away with a lot. But as with all good freedom, this comes with responsibility. You can decide to cheat but you have to make up for it. For instance, if you had some pizza, you could skip a meal to restore the balance. What happens if you disregard this balance? Yes, you end up right back where you started, and most times, in a worse state.

Try to keep the following in mind as you succeed on this journey:

- Eat just enough (nothing more) calories

- Ensure that your diet and overall lifestyle produces low levels of stress for your body
- Supplements turn poisonous when they are taken in high doses, but help your body optimization in low doses.
- A continuously high rate of metabolism is bad for your body, so eat less animal protein and fewer calories.

Made in the USA
San Bernardino, CA
31 May 2019